Be Empowered!

Eat Chocolate with Breakfast

Published by Janbeth Designs

www.janbethdesigns.com

ISBN-13: 978-0-9815229-2-0

Artwork and Book Design — Jan Bethancourt

The paper used in this publication meets the requirements of the American National Standard for Permanence of Paper for Printed Library Materials Z39.48-1984.

Printed in China

The heart and soul of this book is dedicated
with love and admiration to my daughter

Sarah

You are worthy of goodness

Acknowledgments

My loving family makes life a joy. My daughter Sarah's confidence, courage, and compassion unceasingly inspire me. Best friend and husband, Bob, reminds me to enjoy the journey and walks always by my side. Precious to me, my son Jim and his young family provide love, hugs, and a beautiful glimpse of the future. An unfailing positive perspective on life is a unifying trait for my siblings: Judy, Cindi, Hank, Pam, Pat, and Sandy. The gregarious attitude and determined spirit of my mom, Gerry Lacey, is a joyous and powerful influence in all our lives.

Neighbors and friends, old and new, brighten each day. Their loving friendship and support are gifts I treasure. My heartfelt thanks to Kim Baker, not only for friendship but for her artistic insight and technical expertise so generously shared. Sincere gratitude to Robin Roberts, whose quiet kindness and courageous attitude inspired me to broaden the path of this journey. "Courage becomes compassion when it inspires confidence in others."

Thanks to all who have shaped and shared this amazing journey.

Introduction

Dear Reader,

This collection of original sayings began as email messages to my daughter, Sarah, during her years of college. I encouraged her to believe in herself, to stare hardships in the eye, and to know that kindness is not only to be given, but to be graciously accepted as well.

For me, chocolate is a metaphor for confidence, courage, and compassion. My hope is that the sayings in this collection will inspire you to a greater sense of self-worth and an expanded appreciation of all around you.

Life isn't always easy. It is, however, a great deal more rewarding when you have a good attitude, a genuine relationship with your Creator, and a little "chocolate" with breakfast.

Blessings and chocolate,

Jan Bethancourt

Chocolate is—a metaphor for
attitude, confidence, courage, and compassion.

Be Empowered!

Attitude

Be empowered
by the chocolate of life...

Attitude is—an expression of how you see life; yours and life in general.

Your Attitude Defines You

You are worthy of goodness.

The world is more beautiful when viewed through a smile.

Happiness and good fortune usually occur when you are prepared to recognize and receive them.

Celebrate even the smallest joys in your day-to-day existence. Be it with a smile, a song, a hug, or a prayer—celebrate!

Don't wait for a shooting star to make a wish.

Happiness is a choice, peace is possible.
Discover them personally, promote them globally.

Be aware, be appreciative, be amazed by life.

Disappointment is only as profound as you allow it to be.

Difficulties often present you with an opportunity
to welcome wisdom, to practice patience, and to consider change.

Change is inevitable. Accept the old and embrace the new.
Blend the two and that is you.

Courage becomes compassion
when it inspires confidence in another.

Give a powerful gift. Influence self-worth in someone today.

Your positive attitude inspires others
to discover the best in themselves.

Believe you can do anything
and you will accomplish much.

Hug life with arms wide, wide open!
Take it all in. Greet each day with enthusiasm.

Stand in the wind and feel the breeze upon your face.
Know that your Creator has gently embraced you.

Every day is trash day somewhere.
Leave your garbage by the curb.
Start over—free of all the useless stuff.

Breathe deeply. Lay anxiety aside. Focus on gratitude,
recognize opportunity, assess possibility. Breathe deeply!

The peace, purpose, and pleasure
of your life can be realized in the mindful living
and thoughtful giving of each day.

Know yourself, like yourself, love yourself.

Work on an attitude that is positive.
Keep your smile genuine.
Analyze your feelings for the truth.
Closely consider your decisions before acting.
Teach your mind to be flexible, train your body to be strong.
Allow your spirit to be free, nurture your soul to find peace.
Concerning those dear to you—love unconditionally.

Greet each day with an attitude of confidence, courage, and compassion.

You are empowered
...by a healthy **attitude.**

confidence

Be empowered
by the chocolate of awareness...

Confidence is—reliance, trust, and belief in one's self.

Never Underestimate
a Woman and Her Chocolate

Recognize your gifts, identify your goals,
and trust your abilities.

Believe your worthy goals are attainable.

Share your imagination, give voice to your creativity, and cultivate your talents. Express yourself!

Honor your uniqueness!

A small voice can make a great noise.
Do not be silent when you have something of value to share.
Never feel insignificant.

♥

Never doubt your power to affect change in the world
around you.

♥

Shout your dreams to the heavens.
Work like hell to make them come true!

Identifying a problem is the greater part of solving it.

Instead of asking "What's wrong with me?" ask
"How can I be better?"

Do not give in to self-doubt. Believe in yourself
as much as your Creator believes in you!

Set aside what does not work. Search for what works better!

♥

Gently exfoliate the negatives in your life
that keep the best of you from shining through.

♥

Adapting is not a sign of giving-in or giving-up.
It is wisdom in action.

Hope is—preparing yourself to accept any outcome
while believing the best result is possible.

Confidence is a gift you must give yourself.

You are constantly changing, growing, and becoming.
Love yourself along the way. Believe in you.

When you speak to God,
you invite a response from God. Listen!

Appreciate who you are today. Discover, with joy,
the beauty of all you are yet to become.

Look into your heart and soul and see your very best self.
Allow the world to know and see
the wondrous woman you were created to be.

Surprise yourself!
Set your goals beyond what you think you can achieve.
Reach farther than you can grasp.
You are more than you give yourself credit for being.

Chin up, shoulders back, keep moving forward.
Be aware of the beauty of all that you are.

You are empowered
...by **confidence.**

Courage

Be empowered
by the chocolate of knowledge...

Courage is—meeting the challenges of daily life despite your doubts, your fears, and your anxieties.

Chocolate Can Inspire You

♡

With every road you walk, your feet get wiser.

You do not always have the luxury of choosing your journey.
You do have the freedom to choose your own path.

From a distance, a stepping stone and a stumbling block look very much alike. You may not be able to tell which one it is until you are standing on it. In either case, step lightly!

A misstep is not necessarily a mistake.
It could be a pivot point for a new direction!

The most difficult of situations
can become the foundation for a positive transformation.

"What if?" won't change your past.
"What now?" will shape your future.

Seek to know your Maker, and along the journey
you will meet your truest self.

Challenges urge you to recognize the wealth-of-self residing deep within you.

Sometimes you are not appreciated because of what you stand for though secretly admired for taking a stand for what you believe in.

You are remembered, not for the questions you are asked, but for the answers you give.

Heroes are ordinary people who, in a time of crisis,
make extraordinary choices.

Be truthful with yourself.
Be true to yourself.
Be a princess of truth.

Your struggles can make you stronger and wiser.
Your joys can give you hope.
If you accept them, strength, wisdom, and hope
are the gifts of everyday living.

Appreciate where you have been.
It takes you where you are going.

Every day holds powerful potential and profound possibility.
Embrace the future with your heart,
your soul, and your whole being.

Your smile will light your way.
Confidence and courage will direct you.
A joy of life will lift you when you fall.
You love of God will bring you peace.

Perceive the world with all your senses.
See the old in new ways and the new with greater joy.

Listen most closely in silence.
Look most carefully in darkness.
Touch most gently that which is fragile.
Speak always from your heart.

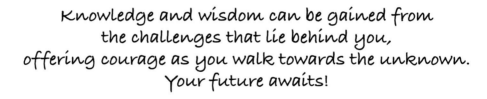

Knowledge and wisdom can be gained from
the challenges that lie behind you,
offering courage as you walk towards the unknown.
Your future awaits!

Recognize the very best of who you are.
Embrace the knowledge that you are
capable of handling any situation.

You are empowered
...by **courage.**

Compassion

Be empowered
by the chocolate of kindness...

Compassion is—a willingness to comfort and can be expressed in ways great or small.

Chocolate, When Shared, Tastes Twice as Sweet

Selflessness leads to self-discovery.

With grace, graciousness and gratitude make kindness a habit.

♥

You give, someone receives.
Consider the magic in that transaction.
Tangible, emotional, or spiritual—your gift
goes beyond the moment.

Step outside your comfort zone. Offer a kind word
or a sincere compliment to someone who would expect it least.

Let the light of your smile shine brightly.
Create a rainbow in someone's rainy day.

Compassion shown to another is a gift you give yourself.

The smile you give someone
may be the only one they get all day. Give generously.

♥

Listen with your ears.
Hear with your heart.
Respond from your soul.

Friends accept where you have been,
acknowledge who you are now, and allow you room to grow.

Like raindrops on a hot day,
friends perk up your parched spirit and flood you with
an abundance of what you need.

Carefully planted words of encouragement are seeds of hope.
Share them, receive them, and watch them bloom.

Goodness and kindness given away are not depleted,
rather, are replenished in the sharing.

♥

Compassion is a gift you offer another,
just as graciously accepting kindness is a gift.

♥

Friends are there to kiss your skinned knees.
Let them. Then two people feel better!

Being compassionate is a way
of sharing the Spirit that resides within you.

A quiet kindness speaks loudly, one word at a time.

It is better to occasionally think a little too well of yourself
than to *ever* doubt your worth.

Discover a peaceful heart and a calm spirit.
Let go of anger and anxiety. Release fear and frustration.
Step away from self–doubt.
At the end of each day, look back with joy
and with gratitude.
As if with the arms of your Creator,
wrap yourself in compassion.

You are worthy of goodness.

Love selflessly.
Live your days with an appreciation
of your Creator, of yourself, and of others.

You are empowered
...by compassion!

Your being is a triangle consisting of body, mind, and spirit.
Each part is dependent on the others for balance and support.
Nourish and strengthen all that you are. Discover peace.

Embrace life with an attitude of confidence, courage, and compassion

You are Empowered!